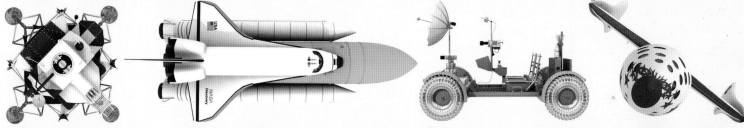

MACHINES CLOSE-UP

SPACE VEHICLES

Daniel Gilpin and Alex Pang

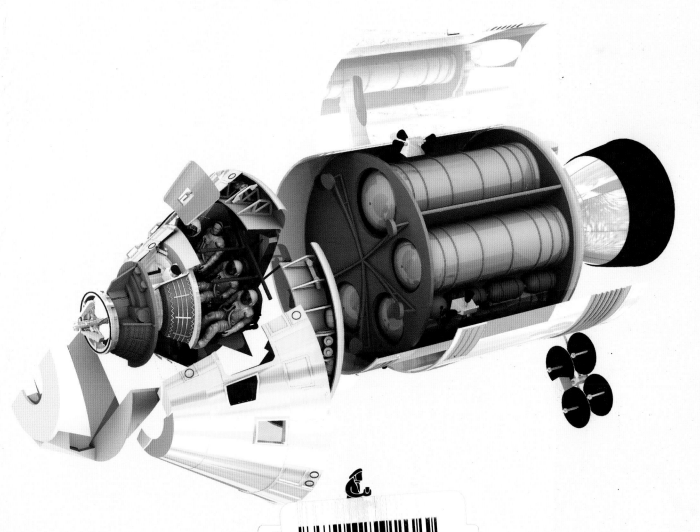

This edition published in 2012 by Wayland

Wayland
Hachette Children's Books
338 Euston Road
London NW1 3BH

Wayland Australia
Level 17/207 Kent Street
Sydney, NSW 2000

Produced by

David West Children's Books
7 Princeton Court
55 Felsham Road
London SW15 1AZ

Designer: Gary Jeffrey
Illustrator: Alex Pang
Editor: Katharine Pethick
Consultant: Steve Parker

A CIP catalogue record for this book is available from the British Library.

ISBN: 9780750269148

Printed in China

Wayland is a division of Hachette Children's Books, an Hachette UK company.
www.hachette.co.uk

PHOTO CREDITS :
Abbreviations: t-top, m-middle, b-bottom, r-right, l-left, c-centre.
4-9 all images courtesy of NASA except 6tl, Retromoderns; 7tl, p_a_h; 30 all images courtesy of NASA

CONTENTS

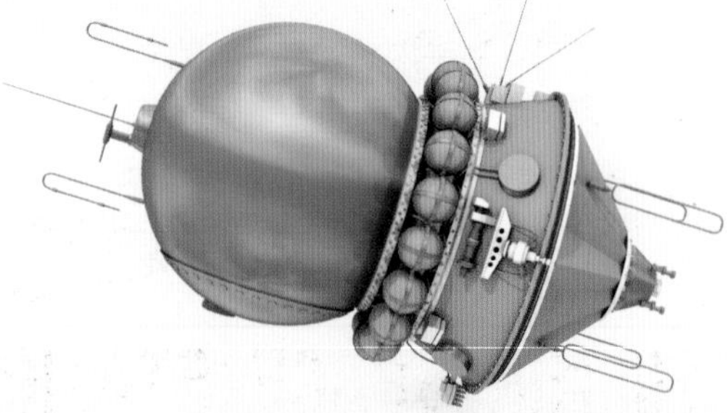

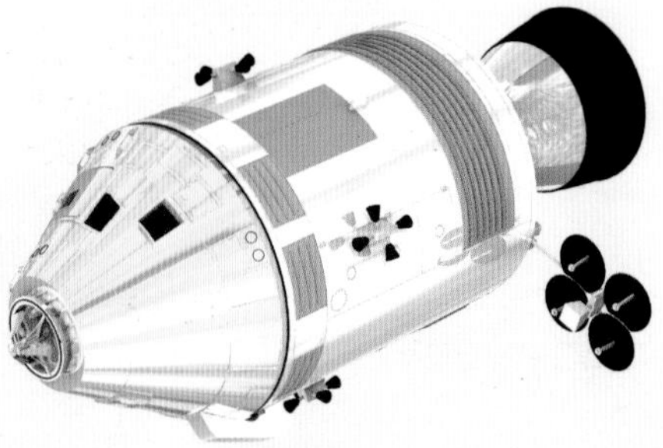

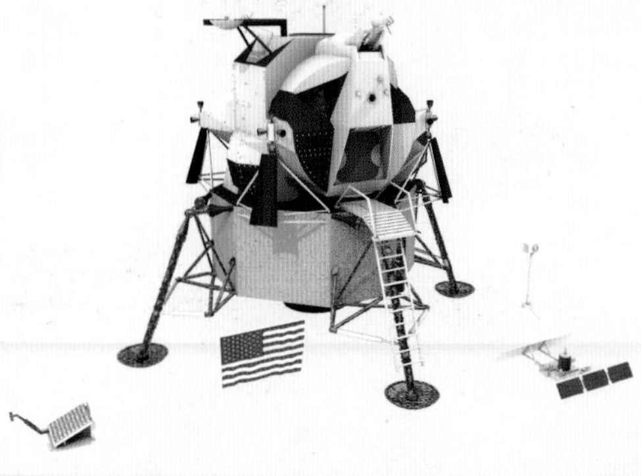

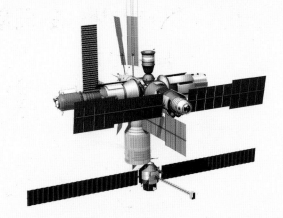

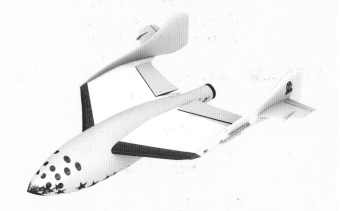

INTRODUCTION

Not so long ago space vehicles were pure science fiction. Today they are a reality and one that has a greater impact on our lives than we might know. Without them there would be no satellite TV, GPS or hurricane warnings. In the future they may affect us even more.

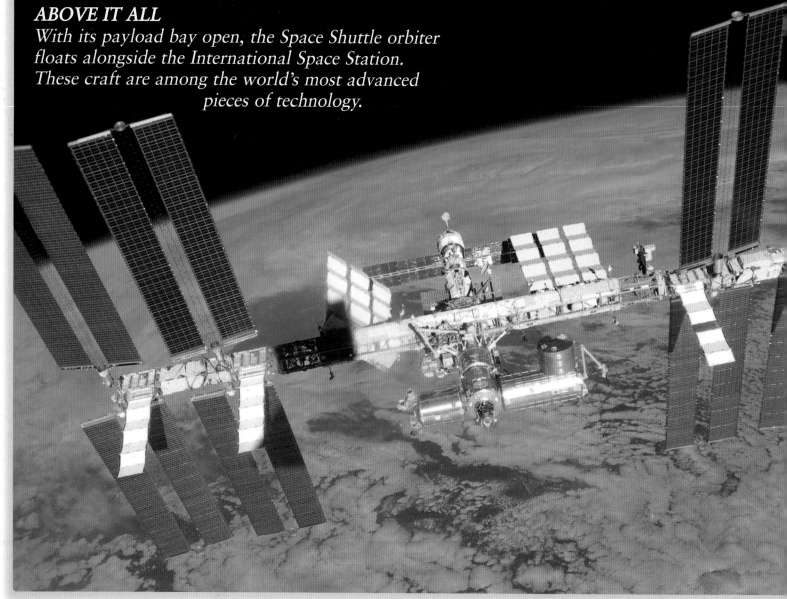

ABOVE IT ALL
With its payload bay open, the Space Shuttle orbiter floats alongside the International Space Station. These craft are among the world's most advanced pieces of technology.

HOW THIS BOOK WORKS

SPECS
This panel gives information about the vehicle's capacity and dimensions.

MAIN TEXT
Explains the function of the vehicle and outlines the history of its use. Other information, such as which nations developed the vehicle, is also covered here.

INTERESTING FEATURES
This box may contain text and illustrations explaining how the vehicle works. Alternatively, it may look in greater detail at one aspect of the vehicle or its mission.

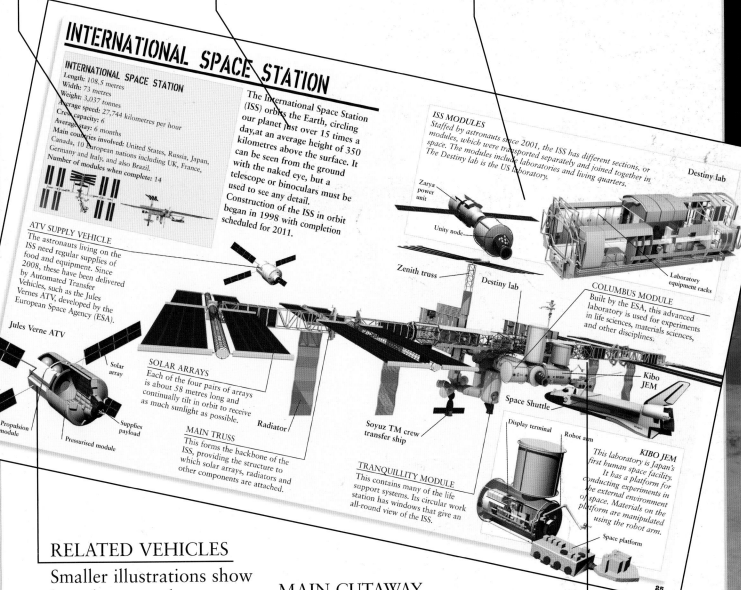

INTERNATIONAL SPACE STATION

INTERNATIONAL SPACE STATION
Length: 108.5 metres
Width: 73 metres
Weight: 3,037 tonnes
Average speed: 27,744 kilometres per hour
Crew capacity: 6
Average stay: 6 months
Main countries involved: United States, Russia, Japan, Canada, 10 European nations including UK, France, Germany and Italy, and also Brazil.
Number of modules when complete: 14

The International Space Station (ISS) orbits the Earth, circling our planet just over 15 times a day, at an average height of 350 kilometres above the surface. It can be seen from the ground with the naked eye, but a telescope or binoculars must be used to see any detail. Construction of the ISS in orbit began in 1998 with completion scheduled for 2011.

ISS MODULES
Staffed by astronauts since 2001, the ISS has different sections, or modules, which were transported separately and joined together in space. The modules include laboratories and living quarters. The Destiny lab is the US laboratory.

Destiny lab

Zarya power unit

Unity node

Laboratory equipment racks

ATV SUPPLY VEHICLE
The astronauts living on the ISS need regular supplies of food and equipment. Since 2008, these have been delivered by Automated Transfer Vehicles, such as the Jules Vernes ATV, developed by the European Space Agency (ESA).

Jules Verne ATV

Propulsion module

Pressurised module

Supplies payload

Solar array

Zenith truss

Destiny lab

Radiator

SOLAR ARRAYS
Each of the four pairs of arrays is about 58 metres long and continually tilt in orbit to receive as much sunlight as possible.

MAIN TRUSS
This forms the backbone of the ISS, providing the structure to which solar arrays, radiators and other components are attached.

Soyuz TM crew transfer ship

TRANQUILLITY MODULE
This contains many of the life support systems. Its circular work station has windows that give an all-round view of the ISS.

COLUMBUS MODULE
Built by the ESA, this advanced laboratory is used for experiments in life sciences, materials sciences, and other disciplines.

Kibo JEM

Space Shuttle

Display terminal

Robot arm

KIBO JEM
This laboratory is Japan's first human space facility. It has a platform for conducting experiments in the external environment of space. Materials on the platform are manipulated using the robot arm.

Space platform

24

25

RELATED VEHICLES
Smaller illustrations show launchers or other vehicles that are used with the main vehicle shown. Alternatively, they may show similar spacecraft.

MAIN CUTAWAY
This exploded illustration shows the internal structure of the vehicle and gives information on the positions of its various working parts.

BREAKING BARRIERS

In the early 20th century, spaceflight was only a distant dream. During the Second World War, however, developments in rocket science led to space travel becoming a reality.

BELL X-1
In 1947, this American rocket plane was first to fly faster than the speed of sound - an important stage in the race into space.

A-4 ROCKET
Also known as the V-2, this was the world's first ballistic missile and the forerunner of all modern rockets.

FIRST SPACE VEHICLES
Spaceflight began in 1944, when a German A-4 rocket left the atmosphere before falling back to Earth. The A-4 was not actually designed to be a space vehicle. The first real space vehicles were developed in the Soviet Union.

SPUTNIK 1
In 1957 this unmanned Soviet craft became the first artificial satellite to orbit the Earth. The launch of Sputnik 1 struck fear into the USA and sparked the beginning of the Space Race.

EXPLORER 1
The first US satellite

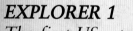

PASSENGERS
Following the success of Sputnik 1, plans were made to put a man in orbit. The first creature to orbit the Earth was a dog called Laika. She went into space aboard Sputnik 2 in 1957, but died during during the mission.

FIRST SPACEMAN
Yuri Gagarin was the first human in space. He orbited the Earth aboard the Soviet craft Vostok 1 in April 1961.

MERCURY CAPSULE

Mercury was America's answer to Vostok 1. In 1962 it succeeded in putting a man into orbit.

JOHN GLENN

He was the first American to orbit Earth.

CIRCLING THE EARTH

After Laika, the Soviets sent several more dogs into orbit while the technology for successful human spaceflight was perfected. In 1961, Yuri Gagarin orbited the Earth, spending more than an hour in space before re-entry.

SPACEWALKS

Gagarin and Glenn remained in their capsules throughout their flights. The next stage in the Space Race was to see who would be the first to walk in space. The Soviets won but the USA followed a few months later with Gemini 4.

VOSKHOD 2

This 1965 Soviet mission saw Alexei Leonov make the first spacewalk. He stayed outside the craft for a full 12 minutes.

GEMINI 4

OTHER WORLDS

With space conquered, the next target was other worlds. The nearest astral body to our planet is the Moon and in the second half of the 1960s both the USA and the Soviet Union planned to be the first to reach it.

MOON MISSIONS

In 1961, President John F Kennedy said 'We choose to go to the Moon'. While the USA was not the first to reach the Moon, it was the first and only nation to land people on it. In 1959, the unmanned Soviet probe, Luna 1, made the first fly-by of the Moon. Later that year another probe, Luna 2, landed on it. The Soviets sent several more probes to the Moon, putting some into orbit around it. In 1969, however, their achievements were topped by the USA when Apollo 11 landed.

SATURN V ROCKET
These enormous rockets propelled the US Apollo astronauts into space and began their missions to the Moon.

MOON WALKER
The first man on the Moon was Neil Armstrong. He was followed by another 11 US astronauts in six missions.

APOLLO CAPSULE
This brought the Apollo astronauts back to Earth. After re-entry, parachutes were deployed for a landing on water.

SPACE PROBES

Since the Moon landings, unmanned probes have been sent to other worlds. Some have performed fly-by missions, whilst others have landed and sent information about planetary surfaces back to Earth. Venus was the first planet to receive a probe on its surface – by the Soviet craft Venera 3 in 1966.

LUNOKHOD 1
The first roving space vehicle

VIKING 2 LANDER
The US Viking missions sent detailed images from the surface of Mars, showing it as a dry and apparently lifeless planet.

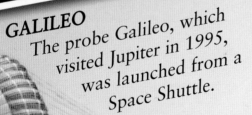

SKYLAB

GALILEO
The probe Galileo, which visited Jupiter in 1995, was launched from a Space Shuttle.

SPACE WORK

Space stations such as the US Skylab have allowed astronauts to spend long periods of time in space and carry out scientific experiments. The Space Shuttle was developed partly to transport astronauts and materials to space stations.

SHUTTLE ORBITER
The Space Shuttle orbiter lands on a runway like a plane. A parachute slows it down when it lands.

VOSTOK 1

Vostok 1 was the world's first manned spacecraft, carrying the Russian cosmonaut Yuri Gagarin into orbit around the Earth on 12 April 1961. Vostok 1 circled the Earth once before re-entering the atmosphere. Seven kilometres from the Earth's surface, Gagarin ejected from the craft, gently descending into a field by parachute.

Gagarin ejects from the re-entry module.

VOSTOK RE-ENTRY

The re-entry of Vostok 1 did not go to plan. After release, the re-entry module remained attached to the rest of the spacecraft by a bundle of wires, only breaking away as these burned up. The re-entry module span wildly, but Gagarin ejected safely.

Ejector hatch

Antenna

Yuri Gagarin

RE-ENTRY MODULE

This sphere was where Yuri Gagarin sat throughout the mission, before he ejected. Upon re-entry it broke away from the main body of Vostok 1.

Clamp bracket

Ejector seat

RELEASE CLAMPS

During lift-off and orbit these held the re-entry module tightly to the main body of Vostok 1. As the spacecraft descended towards Earth they were opened, although the re-entry module remained attached by wires.

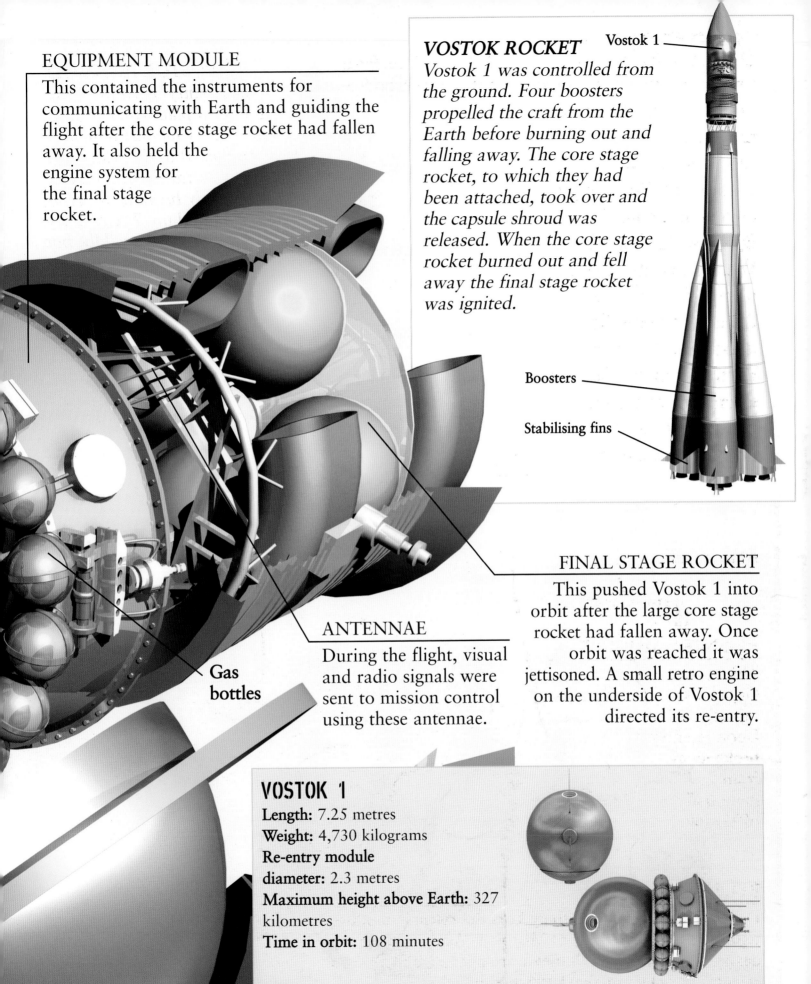

EQUIPMENT MODULE

This contained the instruments for communicating with Earth and guiding the flight after the core stage rocket had fallen away. It also held the engine system for the final stage rocket.

VOSTOK ROCKET

Vostok 1 was controlled from the ground. Four boosters propelled the craft from the Earth before burning out and falling away. The core stage rocket, to which they had been attached, took over and the capsule shroud was released. When the core stage rocket burned out and fell away the final stage rocket was ignited.

Vostok 1

Boosters

Stabilising fins

Gas bottles

ANTENNAE

During the flight, visual and radio signals were sent to mission control using these antennae.

FINAL STAGE ROCKET

This pushed Vostok 1 into orbit after the large core stage rocket had fallen away. Once orbit was reached it was jettisoned. A small retro engine on the underside of Vostok 1 directed its re-entry.

VOSTOK 1

Length: 7.25 metres
Weight: 4,730 kilograms
Re-entry module diameter: 2.3 metres
Maximum height above Earth: 327 kilometres
Time in orbit: 108 minutes

APOLLO COMMAND & SERVICE MODULE

The Apollo missions took American astronauts to the Moon. The final descent was made by the Lunar Module (see overleaf), but during the journey the astronauts travelled in the Command and Service Module (CSM). After the Apollo missions ended, NASA used the CSM in other missions.

HEAT SHIELD

This side of the command module bore most of the friction as it re-entered Earth's atmosphere. The heat shield prevented it from burning up.

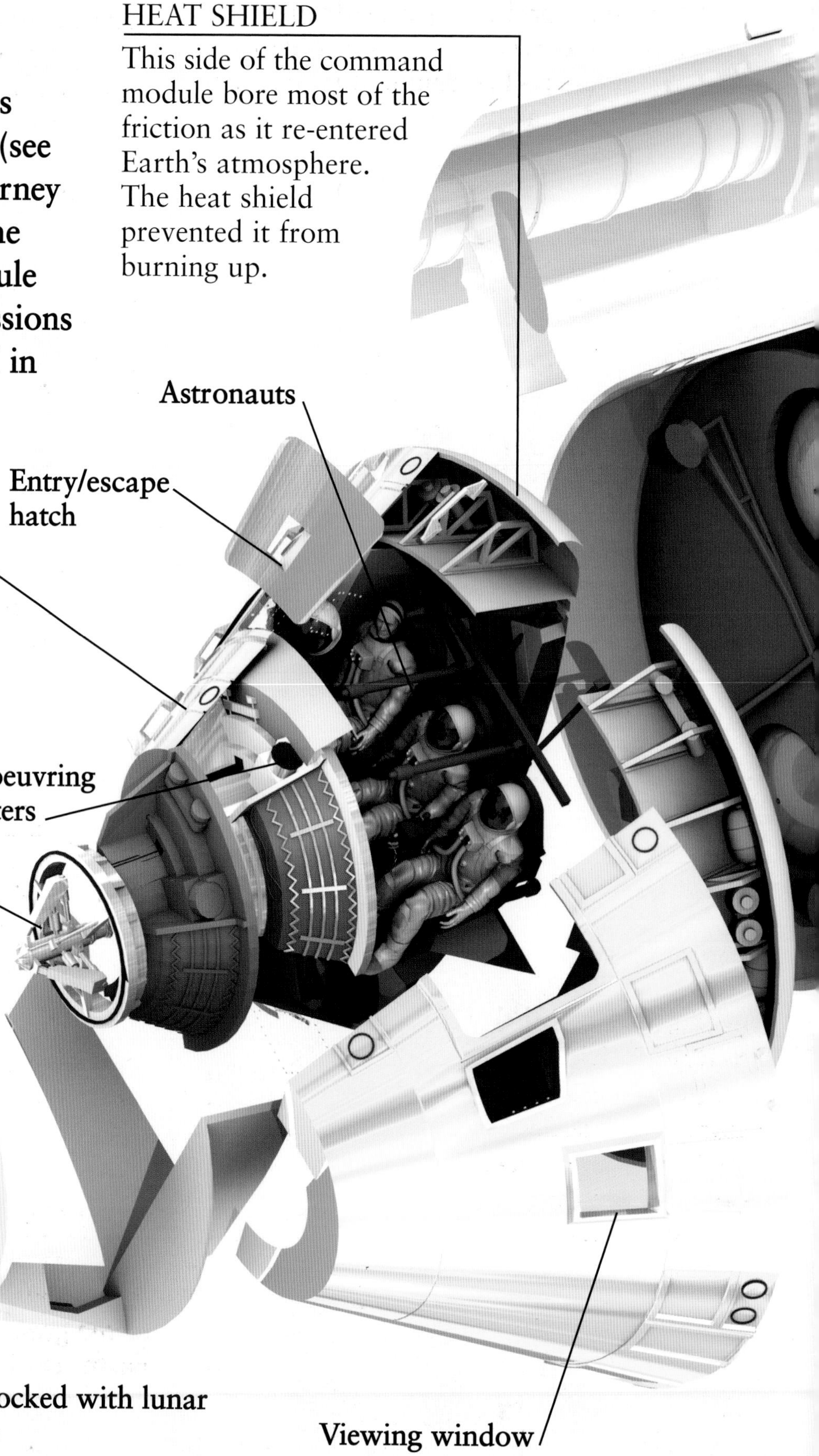

Astronauts

Entry/escape hatch

Manoeuvring thrusters

COMMAND MODULE

This is where the astronauts sat. One of them remained here while the others were on the Moon. He had to pilot the CSM during docking of the Lunar Module.

DOCKING CLAMP

This is where the Lunar Module attached after returning from the Moon. The astronauts entered through a hatch in the middle of the clamp.

CSM docked with lunar module

Viewing window

SERVICE MODULE ENGINE

This propelled the CSM into and out of lunar orbit. It also made mid-course corrections between the Moon and Earth. The engine used AeroZine 50 fuel – as did the Lunar Module.

SATURN V ROCKET

In order to propel a spacecraft to the Moon a huge amount of thrust was needed. That thrust was provided by the Saturn V rocket, which remains the most powerful launch vehicle ever used by NASA. With the Apollo spacecraft on top the Saturn V was 111 metres high. It had three stages – essentially three separate rockets stacked on top of each other. Between them they used up more than 2,000 tonnes of fuel.

Command Module

Escape tower

Service Module

Lunar Module (stored)

Stage three

USA

Stage two

UNITED STATES

MANOEUVRING THRUSTERS

These enabled the CSM to make small adjustments in its position. Their most important job was to align the CSM for docking with the Lunar Module.

Stage one

ANTENNA

The antenna allowed the astronauts to speak to the ground crew on Earth. During launch it was folded flat.

Main engines

APOLLO COMMAND AND SERVICE MODULE

Length: 11 metres
Diameter: 3.9 metres
Weight: 30,330 kilograms
Crew cabin volume: 6.2 cubic metres
Number of crew: 3

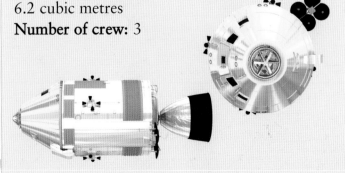

APOLLO LUNAR MODULE

The Apollo Lunar Module was one of the most specialised vehicles ever built. Its job was to take astronauts from the Apollo Command and Service Module, orbiting the Moon, and transfer them to the Moon's surface. On the Moon, it provided living quarters for the astronauts for several days, before returning them to lunar orbit to join the Command and Service Module.

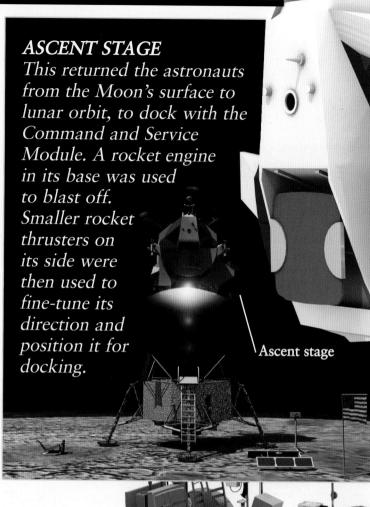

ASCENT STAGE
This returned the astronauts from the Moon's surface to lunar orbit, to dock with the Command and Service Module. A rocket engine in its base was used to blast off. Smaller rocket thrusters on its side were then used to fine-tune its direction and position it for docking.

Ascent stage

Laser Ranging Retroreflector

Passive Seismic Experiment Package

LUNAR SURFACE EXPERIMENTS
During the six Moon landings scientific experiments were carried out, using equipment stored in the lander's descent stage. The Laser Ranging Retroreflector reflected a laser shone from Earth to measure the Moon's distance. The Passive Seismic Experiment Package detected 'moonquakes'.

APOLLO LUNAR MODULE
Height: 6.9 metres
Weight (including fuel): 15 tonnes
Diameter: 4.2 metres
Crew cabin volume: 6.65 cubic metres
Water storage capacity: 190 litres

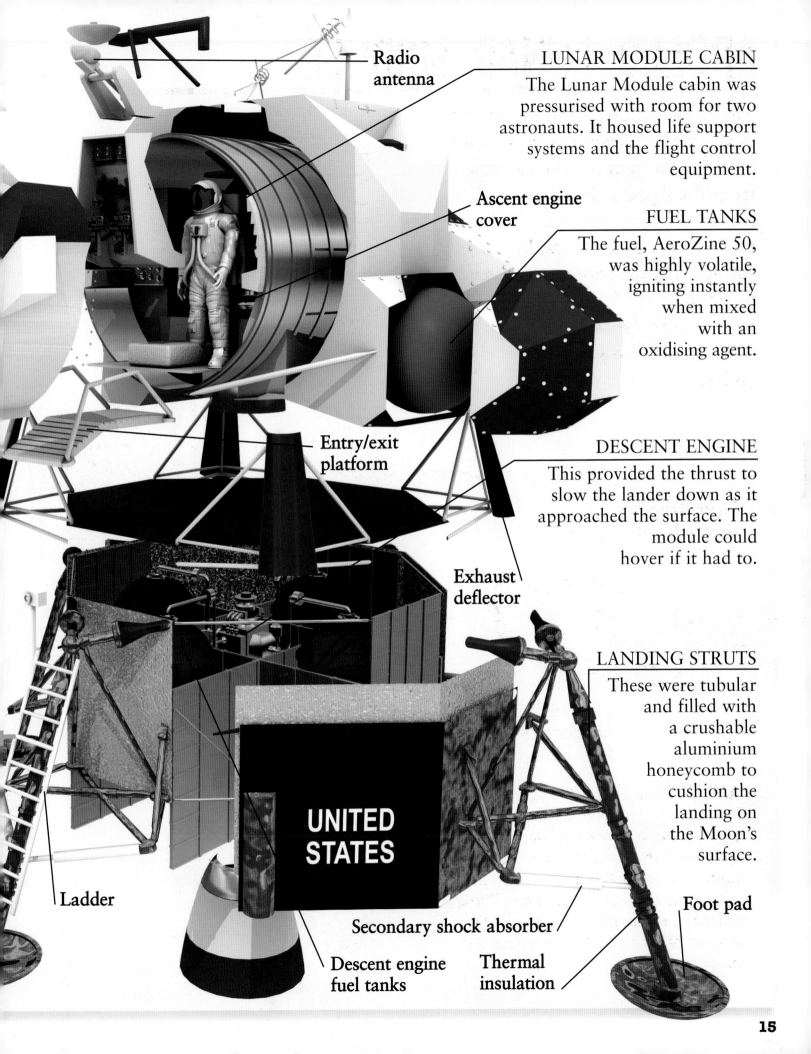

Radio
antenna

LUNAR MODULE CABIN
The Lunar Module cabin was
pressurised with room for two
astronauts. It housed life support
systems and the flight control
equipment.

Ascent engine
cover

FUEL TANKS
The fuel, AeroZine 50,
was highly volatile,
igniting instantly
when mixed
with an
oxidising agent.

Entry/exit
platform

DESCENT ENGINE
This provided the thrust to
slow the lander down as it
approached the surface. The
module could
hover if it had to.

Exhaust
deflector

LANDING STRUTS
These were tubular
and filled with
a crushable
aluminium
honeycomb to
cushion the
landing on
the Moon's
surface.

UNITED
STATES

Ladder

Secondary shock absorber

Descent engine
fuel tanks

Thermal
insulation

Foot pad

LUNAR ROVER

The Lunar Rover was developed so that astronauts could travel further during their three-day stays on the Moon. Lunar Rovers were used on the last three manned missions to the Moon: Apollo 15, Apollo 16 and Apollo 17. They travelled about five kilometres from the Lunar Module.

CONTROLS

The Lunar Rover was controlled by a T-shaped joystick, pushed forward to accelerate and moved left or right to steer. Pulling back on the joystick activated the brakes, unless a separate switch was pressed, which made the Lunar Rover reverse.

16mm movie camera

Low-gain antenna

High-gain antenna

Colour TV camera

COMMUNICATIONS

The Lunar Rover carried several devices used to communicate with the Command and Service Module and Mission Control. The colour TV camera was remotely operated by Mission Control on Earth. It was used not only to film excursions in the Lunar Rover but also the Lunar Module's take-off and ascent at the end of the mission.

Communications relay unit

Control console

POWER PACK

The Lunar Rover was a four-wheel drive electric vehicle. It was powered by two 36-volt silver-zinc potassium hydroxide batteries.

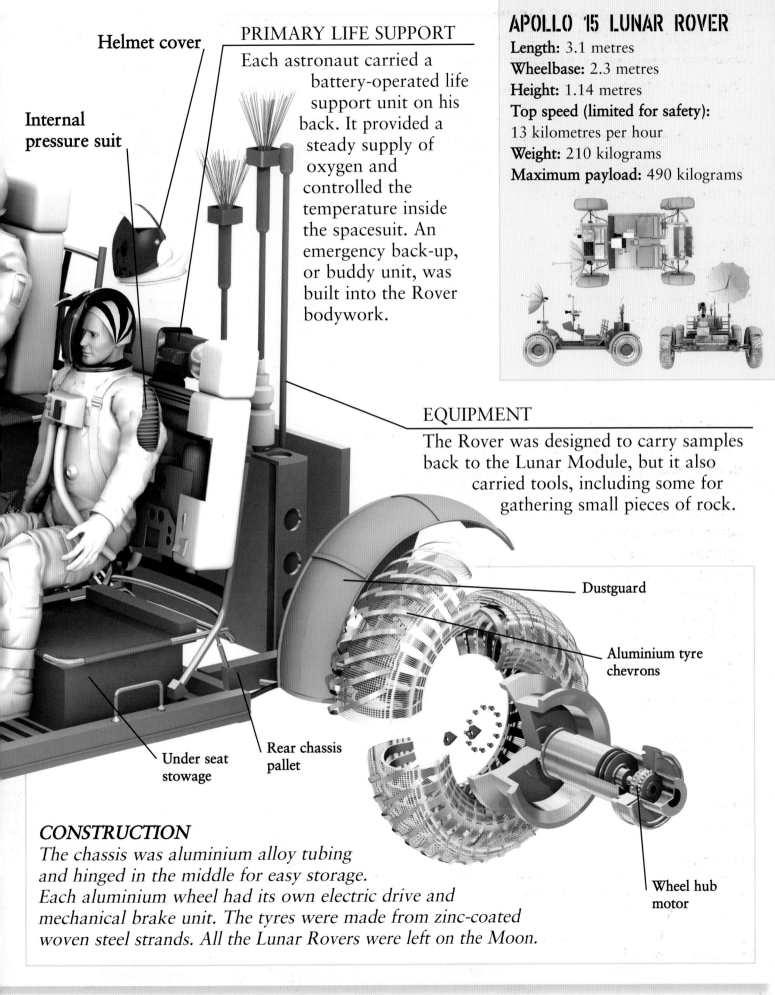

Helmet cover

Internal
pressure suit

PRIMARY LIFE SUPPORT

Each astronaut carried a
battery-operated life
support unit on his
back. It provided a
steady supply of
oxygen and
controlled the
temperature inside
the spacesuit. An
emergency back-up,
or buddy unit, was
built into the Rover
bodywork.

APOLLO 15 LUNAR ROVER

Length: 3.1 metres
Wheelbase: 2.3 metres
Height: 1.14 metres
Top speed (limited for safety):
13 kilometres per hour
Weight: 210 kilograms
Maximum payload: 490 kilograms

EQUIPMENT

The Rover was designed to carry samples
back to the Lunar Module, but it also
carried tools, including some for
gathering small pieces of rock.

Dustguard

Aluminium tyre
chevrons

Under seat
stowage

Rear chassis
pallet

Wheel hub
motor

CONSTRUCTION

*The chassis was aluminium alloy tubing
and hinged in the middle for easy storage.
Each aluminium wheel had its own electric drive and
mechanical brake unit. The tyres were made from zinc-coated
woven steel strands. All the Lunar Rovers were left on the Moon.*

SPACE SHUTTLE

The Space Shuttle was the first partially reuseable spacecraft. It transported payloads into Earth orbit, collected satellites from space and brought them back to Earth, and carried astronauts to and from the International Space Station. Six Space Shuttle orbiter vehicles were built. Five of them carried out missions in space.

PAYLOAD BAY

This forms much of the length of the orbiter vehicle so the Space Shuttle can carry large objects into orbit. The Hubble Space Telescope was deployed in 1990 and has been visited five times by Space Shuttles since.

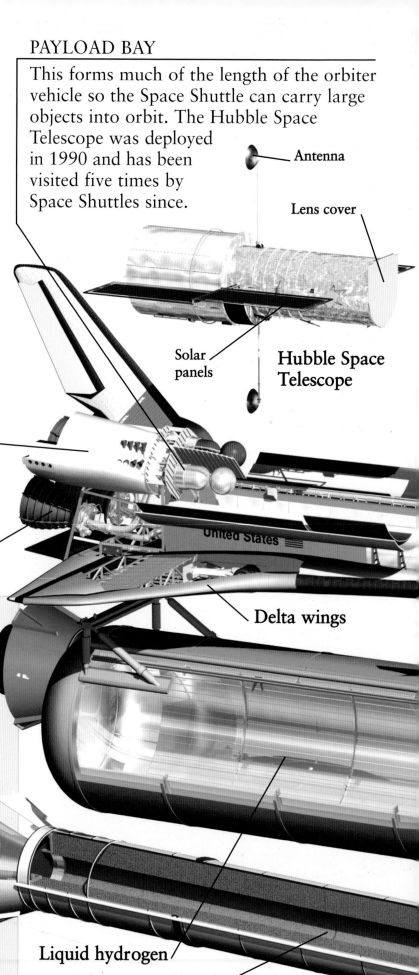

Antenna

Lens cover

Solar panels

Hubble Space Telescope

Main engines

Delta wings

Liquid hydrogen

Solid fuel propellant

ORBITER VEHICLE

This is the main reusable part of the Space Shuttle. As well as operating in space, the orbiter can glide and descend safely to a runway on the Earth's surface.

SHUTTLE ORBITER AND BOOSTER

Total length: 56.1 metres
Total weight: 2,030 tonnes
Orbiter length: 37.2 metres
Orbiter wingspan: 23.8 metres
Operational altitude: 185–1,000 kilometres
Maximum payload: 25,084 kilograms

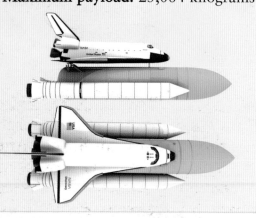

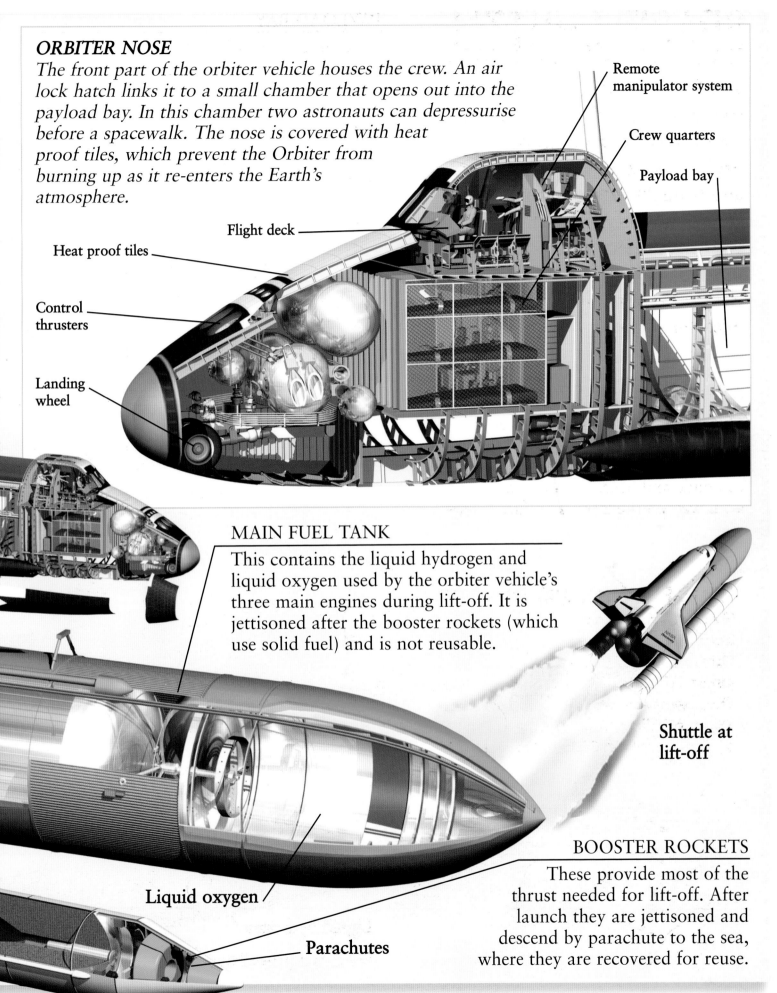

ORBITER NOSE

The front part of the orbiter vehicle houses the crew. An air lock hatch links it to a small chamber that opens out into the payload bay. In this chamber two astronauts can depressurise before a spacewalk. The nose is covered with heat proof tiles, which prevent the Orbiter from burning up as it re-enters the Earth's atmosphere.

Remote manipulator system

Crew quarters

Payload bay

Flight deck

Heat proof tiles

Control thrusters

Landing wheel

MAIN FUEL TANK

This contains the liquid hydrogen and liquid oxygen used by the orbiter vehicle's three main engines during lift-off. It is jettisoned after the booster rockets (which use solid fuel) and is not reusable.

Shuttle at lift-off

Liquid oxygen

Parachutes

BOOSTER ROCKETS

These provide most of the thrust needed for lift-off. After launch they are jettisoned and descend by parachute to the sea, where they are recovered for reuse.

MIR SPACE STATION

Mir was a Russian predecessor to the International Space Station. Its first section was launched into Earth orbit in 1986 where it was visited by two cosmonauts who shuttled across from Salyut-7 – a smaller Russian space station, already in orbit. Its core was added to, enabling Mir to operate for 15 years. In 2001 it was brought out of orbit and crashed into the Pacific Ocean.

SOLAR PANELS
These generated the electricity to power the life support and other vital systems.

MIR SPACE STATION
Weight: 1,243 tonnes
Crew capacity: 3
Total number of crew members: 137
Longest stay: 438 days (Valery Polyakov)
Total time in orbit: 5,511 days
Date first occupied: 15 March 1986
Re-entry: 23 March 2001

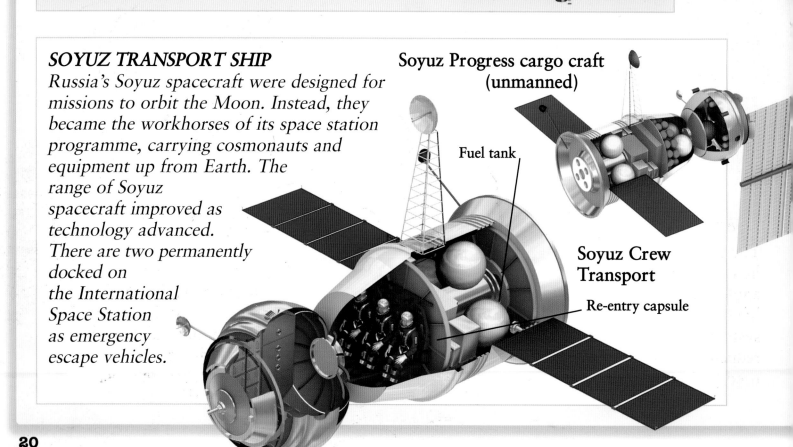

SOYUZ TRANSPORT SHIP
Russia's Soyuz spacecraft were designed for missions to orbit the Moon. Instead, they became the workhorses of its space station programme, carrying cosmonauts and equipment up from Earth. The range of Soyuz spacecraft improved as technology advanced. There are two permanently docked on the International Space Station as emergency escape vehicles.

Soyuz Progress cargo craft (unmanned)

Fuel tank

Soyuz Crew Transport

Re-entry capsule

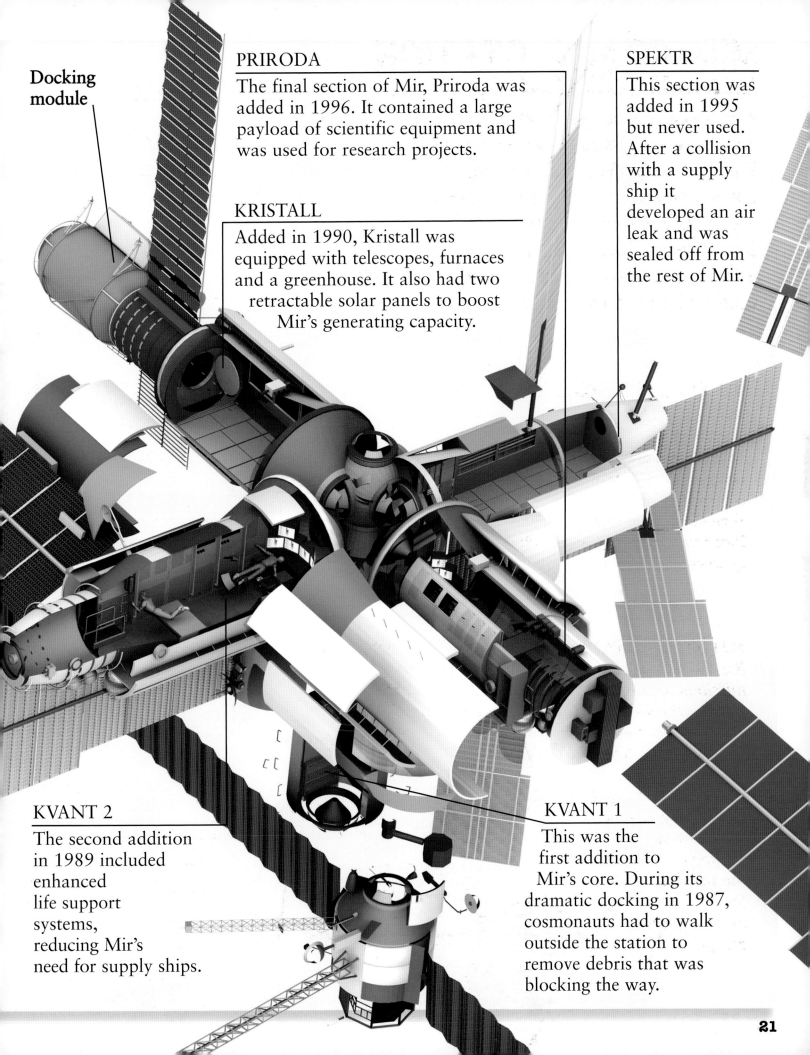

Docking module

PRIRODA

The final section of Mir, Priroda was added in 1996. It contained a large payload of scientific equipment and was used for research projects.

KRISTALL

Added in 1990, Kristall was equipped with telescopes, furnaces and a greenhouse. It also had two retractable solar panels to boost Mir's generating capacity.

SPEKTR

This section was added in 1995 but never used. After a collision with a supply ship it developed an air leak and was sealed off from the rest of Mir.

KVANT 2

The second addition in 1989 included enhanced life support systems, reducing Mir's need for supply ships.

KVANT 1

This was the first addition to Mir's core. During its dramatic docking in 1987, cosmonauts had to walk outside the station to remove debris that was blocking the way.

GPS SATELLITE AND LAUNCH ROCKET

Before Sputnik there were no artificial satellites around Earth. Today there are thousands, involved in everything from weather prediction to television broadcasting. GPS satellites are used for navigation (GPS stands for Global Positioning System). It was developed by the US Department of Defense but is now used by everyone.

ANTENNA ARRAY

This transmits a unique signal that can be detected by a GPS receiver below. A receiver unit must pick up signals from at least three GPS satellites and use the times the signals took to reach it to calculate its position on Earth.

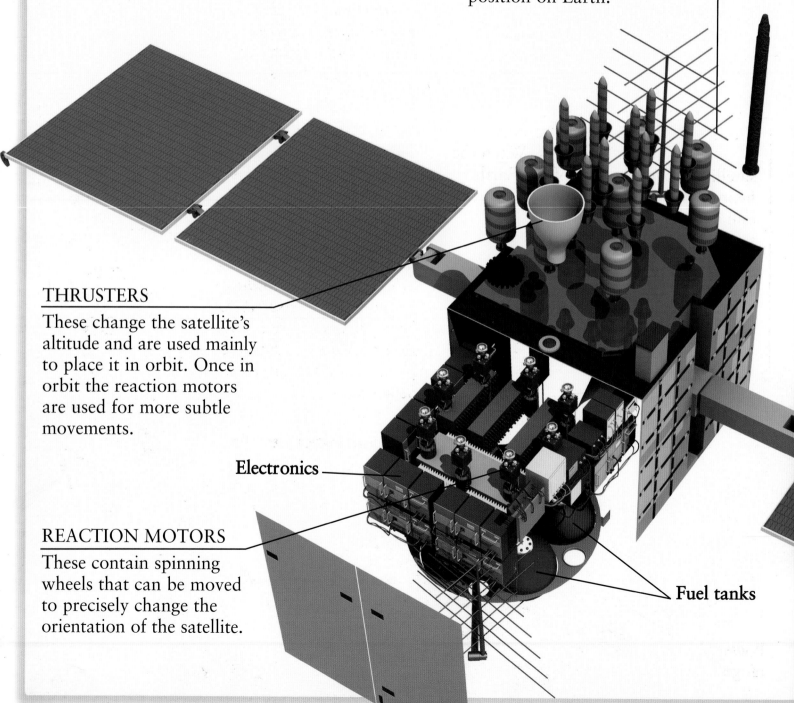

THRUSTERS

These change the satellite's altitude and are used mainly to place it in orbit. Once in orbit the reaction motors are used for more subtle movements.

Electronics

REACTION MOTORS

These contain spinning wheels that can be moved to precisely change the orientation of the satellite.

Fuel tanks

GPS SATELLITE

Length: 1.9 metres
Diameter: 1.93 metres
Solar panel span: 11.4 metres
Weight: 2,032 kilograms
Average active lifespan: 10 years
First launched: 1990

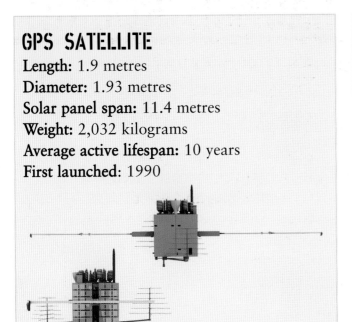

SOLAR PANELS

These turn sunlight into electricity to power the satellite's systems. When the satellite is over the side of the Earth facing away from the Sun (where it is night) power is provided by rechargeable back-up batteries.

NAVSTAR GPS satellite

Solar panels

Powered hinge

SATELLITE LAUNCH VEHICLE

The European Ariane 4 rocket system takes communications and Earth observation satellites into space. Each Ariane rocket is only used once. Once all of the fuel from the first stage has been used up the second stage ignites to carry the payload (which can be up to 4.2 tonnes) into orbit.

Satellite payload stage

Second stage

First stage

Ariane 4 rocket

SATELLITE TYPES

GPS satellites circle the Earth several times a day. Many other satellites, including communications satellites, have geostationary orbits – rotating with the Earth to remain over the same place on its surface.

Communications satellite

Antenna dish

INTERNATIONAL SPACE STATION

INTERNATIONAL SPACE STATION

Length: 108.5 metres
Width: 73 metres
Weight: 3,037 tonnes
Average speed: 27,744 kilometres per hour
Crew capacity: 6
Average stay: 6 months
Main countries involved: United States, Russia, Japan, Canada, 10 European nations including UK, France, Germany and Italy, and also Brazil.
Number of modules when complete: 14

The International Space Station (ISS) orbits the Earth, circling our planet just over 15 times a day, at an average height of 350 kilometres above the surface. It can be seen from the ground with the naked eye, but a telescope or binoculars must be used to see any detail. Construction of the ISS in orbit began in 1998 with completion scheduled for 2011.

ATV SUPPLY VEHICLE

The astronauts living on the ISS need regular supplies of food and equipment. Since 2008, these have been delivered by Automated Transfer Vehicles, such as the Jules Vernes ATV, developed by the European Space Agency (ESA).

Jules Verne ATV

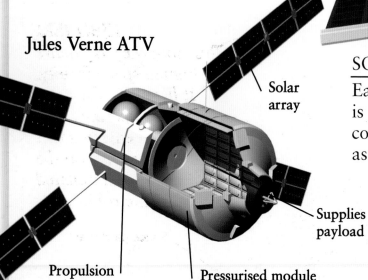

Solar array

Supplies payload

Propulsion module

Pressurised module

SOLAR ARRAYS

Each of the four pairs of arrays is about 58 metres long and continually tilts in orbit to receive as much sunlight as possible.

Radiator

MAIN TRUSS

This forms the backbone of the ISS, providing the structure to which solar arrays, radiators and other components are attached.

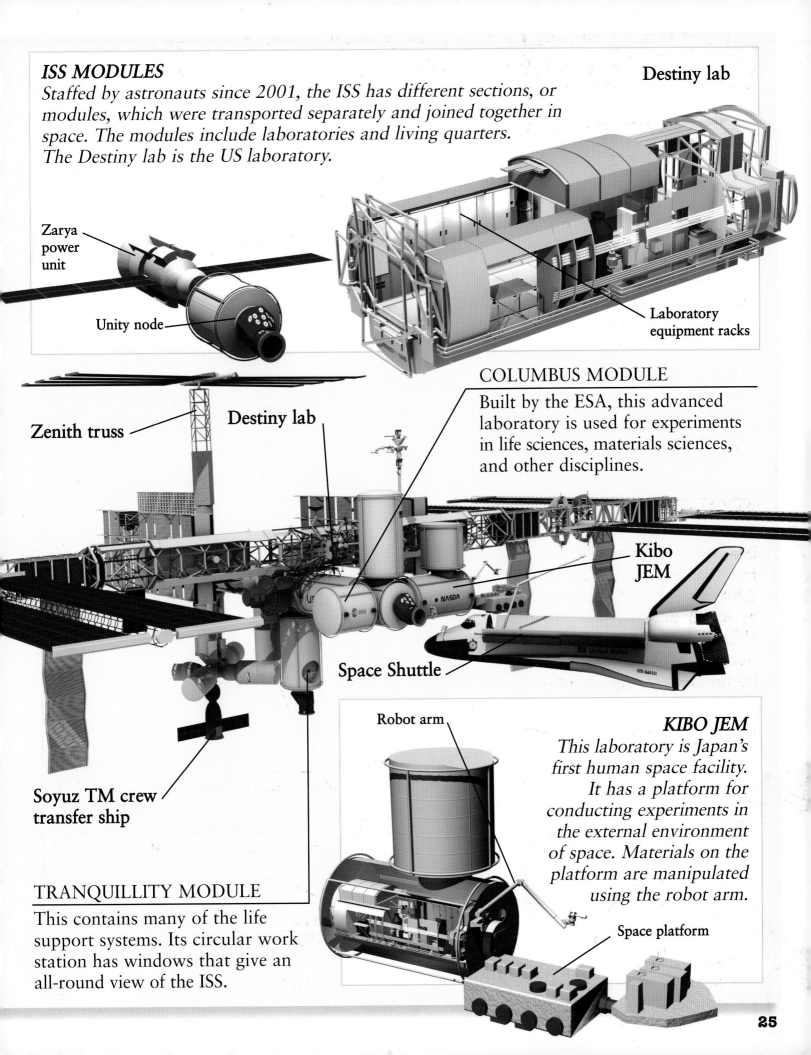

ISS MODULES

Staffed by astronauts since 2001, the ISS has different sections, or modules, which were transported separately and joined together in space. The modules include laboratories and living quarters. The Destiny lab is the US laboratory.

Destiny lab

Zarya power unit

Unity node

Laboratory equipment racks

Zenith truss

Destiny lab

COLUMBUS MODULE

Built by the ESA, this advanced laboratory is used for experiments in life sciences, materials sciences, and other disciplines.

Kibo JEM

Space Shuttle

Soyuz TM crew transfer ship

TRANQUILLITY MODULE

This contains many of the life support systems. Its circular work station has windows that give an all-round view of the ISS.

Robot arm

KIBO JEM

This laboratory is Japan's first human space facility. It has a platform for conducting experiments in the external environment of space. Materials on the platform are manipulated using the robot arm.

Space platform

MARS ROVER

Panoramic cameras

The Mars Rover was designed by NASA to explore the surface of Mars. There have been three successful Mars Rover landings, the first in 1997. Two more were landed in 2004 and are still working there. The Mars Rover was partly inspired by the two Soviet Lunokhod rovers sent to the Moon in the 1970s.

CAMERA MAST

This enables the Rover to 'see' over rocks and other surface obstacles, making it easier to manoeuvre. The panoramic cameras record landscape views.

MARS EXPLORATION ROVER

Length: 1.6 metres
Width: 2.3 metres
Height: 1.5 metres
Weight: 185 kilograms
Top speed: 5 centimetres per second
Names: Spirit (MER-A landed 4 January 2004), Opportunity (MER-B landed 25 January 2004)

SOLAR PANELS

These provide the Rover's electric power and recharge the batteries.

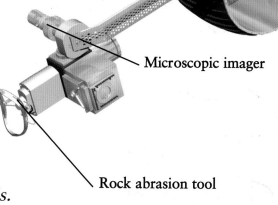

Microscopic imager

ROBOT TOOL ARM

This was designed to operate like a human arm and has an 'elbow' and a 'wrist'. The rock abrasion tool it carries does the same job as a geologist's hammer, exposing the insides of rocks. The microscopic imager provides magnifying views of the insides and outsides of rocks and these are sent back to Earth for analysis.

Rock abrasion tool

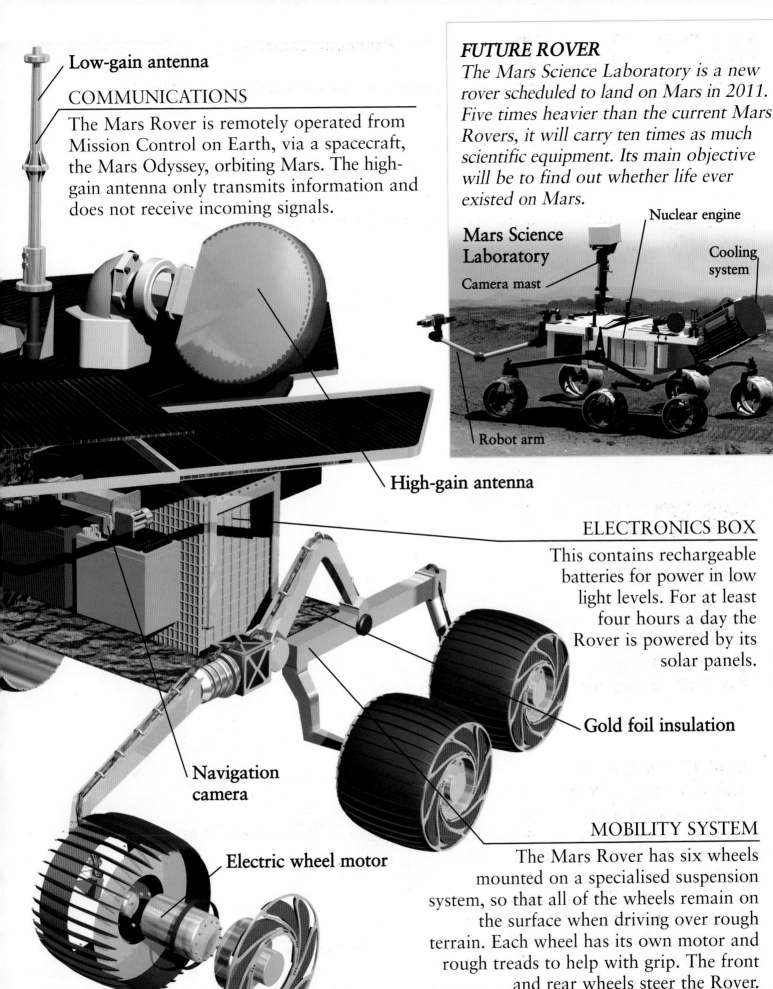

COMMUNICATIONS

Low-gain antenna

The Mars Rover is remotely operated from Mission Control on Earth, via a spacecraft, the Mars Odyssey, orbiting Mars. The high-gain antenna only transmits information and does not receive incoming signals.

High-gain antenna

ELECTRONICS BOX

This contains rechargeable batteries for power in low light levels. For at least four hours a day the Rover is powered by its solar panels.

Navigation camera

Gold foil insulation

Electric wheel motor

MOBILITY SYSTEM

The Mars Rover has six wheels mounted on a specialised suspension system, so that all of the wheels remain on the surface when driving over rough terrain. Each wheel has its own motor and rough treads to help with grip. The front and rear wheels steer the Rover.

SPACESHIPONE

SpaceShipOne is a relatively new development in space travel. On 21 June 2004, it became the first privately-funded manned vehicle to enter space, flying just outside the Earth's atmosphere at an altitude of 100.1 kilometres. Two more flights were made before SpaceShipOne was retired. During the third flight, it reached a maximum altitude of 112 kilometres.

FLIGHT CONTROLS

SpaceShipOne's flight controls were similar to a jet fighter's. A joystick controlled lift and direction. Positioning information was sent via a digital display console, enabling the pilot to guide the spacecraft back to its landing site.

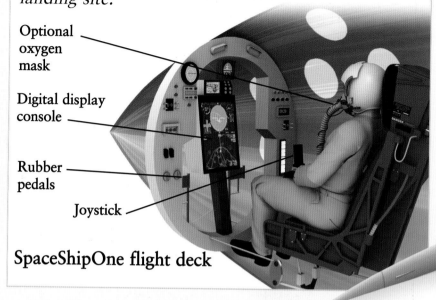

Optional oxygen mask

Digital display console

Rubber pedals

Joystick

SpaceShipOne flight deck

SPACESHIPONE

Wingspan: 5 metres
Length: 5 metres
Weight: 1,200 kilograms
Propellant: Nitrous oxide and rubber hybrid rocket fuel
Top speed: 3,518 kilometres per hour
Crew: 1 (total capacity 2)

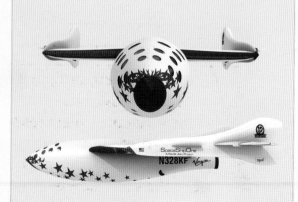

FUSELAGE

Most of the fuselage housed the fuel tank and engine, but the cockpit was quite spacious. The nose cone was removed to let the pilot out.

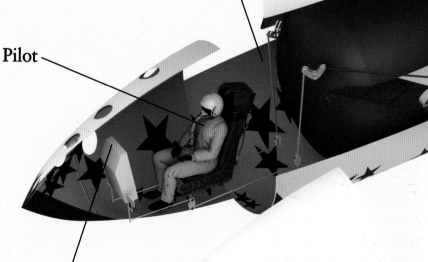

Pilot

Viewing ports

ROCKET MOTOR

This was ignited after the release of SpaceShipOne from White Knight. The pilot pulled SpaceShipOne into an almost vertical trajectory, flying through the edge of the atmosphere before switching off and gliding back down to land.

WHITE KNIGHT MOTHERSHIP

SpaceShipOne was launched at an altitude of 14,326 metres from beneath its mothership, known as White Knight. The forward outer fuselage, cockpit and avionics of White Knight were identical to those of SpaceShipOne. It was powered by turbojet engines rather than a rocket and had two flight pilots.

Turbojets

SpaceShipOne

White Knight with SpaceShipOne

Rudder

Nozzle

Aileron

COMPOSITE SKIN

The outer skin was of a graphite/epoxy composite material, combining lightness with strength.

Wings in re-entry position

VARIABLE WINGS

The wings were designed to change position. During re-entry their rear halves rotated to maximise resistance and slow the craft down.

FUTURE MACHINES

Space exploration has only just begun. There are places in our own Solar System that probes have yet to visit. Future spacecraft will explore these, adding to our knowledge of the worlds that probes have visited already.

Plans to send craft to Mars, Jupiter and its moons, and other worlds are regularly updated by space scientists. NASA has committed itself to returning people to the Moon and building a sustainable base for astronauts to live on its surface. And with the Space Shuttle shortly due to be retired its replacement, the Orion spacecraft, is nearing the final stages of its development.

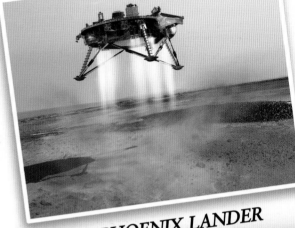

MARS PHOENIX LANDER
This craft reached Mars in 2008 and was the first to land in one of Mars's polar regions.

DC-XA
This craft was developed in the 1990s. Some NASA scientists believe it could be adapted into a manned Mars lander.

ORION CEV/MOON LANDER
This lander is part of NASA's Constellation Project, which aims to take explorers to the Moon and then onward to Mars and other planets.

GLOSSARY

air lock
An airtight chamber, usually between two areas of different pressure. An air lock prevents a spacecraft's air from escaping, as it would if just a single door was opened.

astral body
A planet or other large object in space.

avionics
An abbreviation of 'aviation electronics'. The electrical and electronic systems that enable an aircraft or similar vehicle to fly.

chassis
The rectangular steel frame that forms the basic skeleton of a motor vehicle. The axles and the frame that supports the bodywork are attached to the chassis.

communications satellite
An artificial satellite used for TV and radio broadcasting, telephone calls, computer links and similar communications.

cosmonaut
An astronaut from Russia or the old Soviet Union.

fuselage
The central body of an aeroplane or similar craft, to which the wings and tail are attached.

GPS
Global Positioning System. A system of satellites that allows people with specialised receivers to pinpoint exactly where they are on the Earth.

Hubble Space Telescope
A large telescope that orbits the Earth.

life sciences
Sciences such as botany and zoology that are involved in the study of living things.

mission control
The centre on Earth from which a space mission is monitored or controlled.

NASA
National Aeronautics and Space Administration. The US government agency responsible for the US space programme.

re-entry
The return of a vehicle from space into the Earth's atmosphere.

satellite
An object that orbits, or circles, another object in space. The Moon is a natural satellite of Earth. Artificial satellites are those made by humans (the word satellite is often used to apply simply to these).

Soviet Union
A group of communist countries that included Russia, East Germany, and the Ukraine, among others. The Soviet Union dissolved in 1991.

spacewalk
When astronauts in space put on spacesuits and go outside their spacecraft.

INDEX